AF571757

Berta Broadfoot and Pepin the Short

Berta Broadfoot and Pepin the Short: A Merovingian Romance

by Barbara Goldberg

Wood Engravings by Rosemary Covey

Rosemary Feit Covey

The Porcupine's Quill, Incorporated

Published by the Porcupine's Quill, Inc., 68 Main Street, Erin, Ontario NOB 1TO. Published simultaneously in the United States by The Word Works, P.O. Box 42164, Washington, D.C. 20015. Distributed in Canada by Firefly Books, 3520 Pharmacy Avenue, Unit 1C, Scarborough, Ontario M1W 2T8.

Berta Broadfoot and Pepin the Short was first presented in 1984 at Glen Echo Park, Maryland in the Poet's Jam, a mixed media performance series sponsored by The Word Works. Some of the poems were first published in *Frank* (Paris, France).

The author specially thanks Myra Sklarew, Laura Fargas, Paris C. Pacchione, Janice Olson, and Karren Alenier who first introduced her to Rosemary Covey and her wood engravings.

The engravings appearing in this book may be purchased as original artist's prints by contacting Rosemary Covey, Torpedo Factory, 105 Union Street, Alexandria, VA 22314.

Typeset in Aldus by The Coach House Press (Toronto). Printed on Zephyr Antique laid, sewn into signatures and bound by the Porcupine's Quill, Inc. (Erin).

ISBN 0-88984-102-0

LC 86-50181

for my mother and in memory of her parents,
Friedrich and Blanka Briess

THE MEROVINGIANS

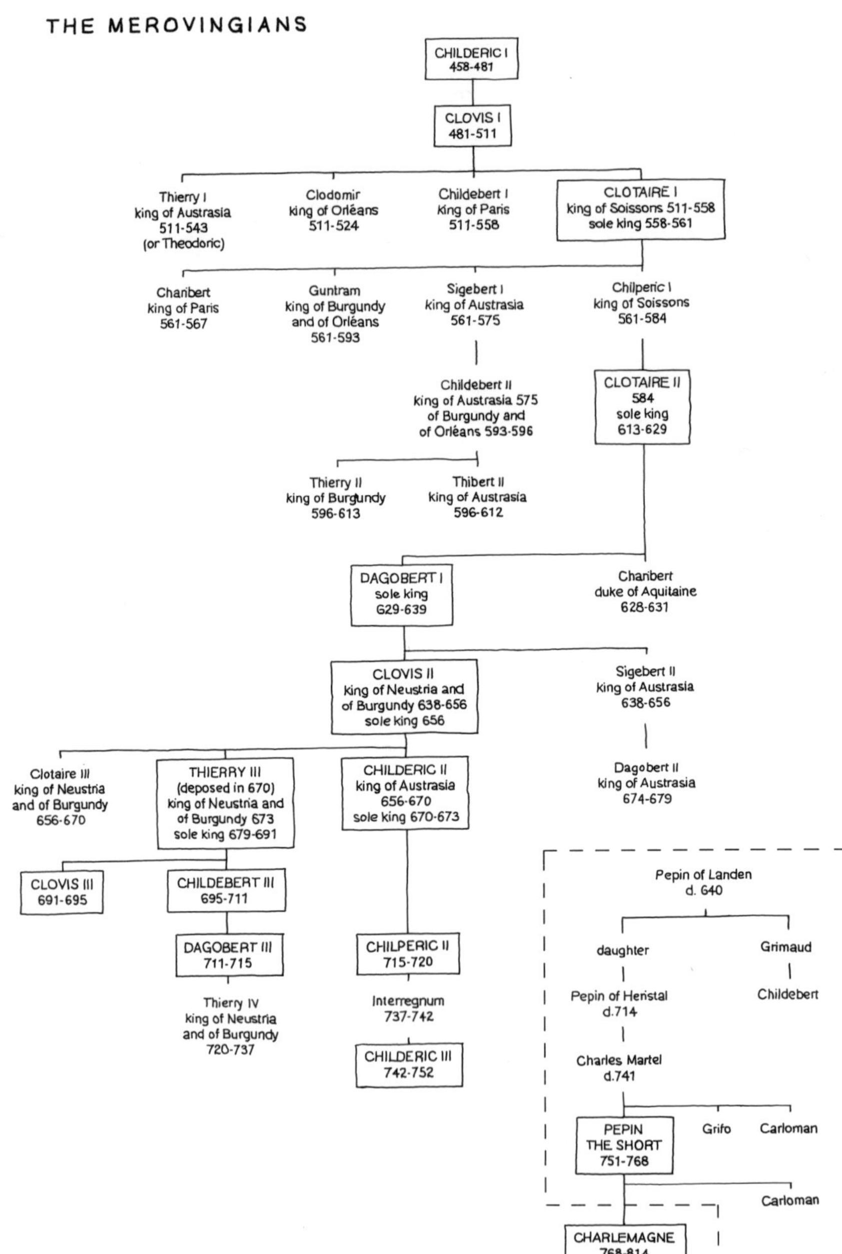

IN FAIRY TALES, different characters can often be viewed as manifestations of the same person. For example, the child's opposing feelings of love and anger for the mother are split into the good fairy godmother and the bad stepmother or witch. Father is similarly split into the good woodcutter and the bad wolf or beast.

In both Eastern and Western literature, woman has been split into the Lady – pure, dutiful, devout – and the Chambermaid – sensuous, primitive, intuitive rather than intellectual. W.B. Yeats has dealt with this theme in his poem 'The Three Bushes'. Here, the 'dumb' (literally, since he never speaks) male is duped. He is unaware that the woman he truly loves and admires is not the woman he sleeps with at night. The Lady has substituted her Chambermaid in bed in order to preserve her own virtue. The male dies, never the wiser.

A woman's attempt to reconcile these two aspects of her nature, the rational and the instinctive, and the complexities of the mother-daughter relationship are what drew me to the myth of Berta of Hungary. I stumbled upon the story when I bought *Medieval Myths* by Norma Lorre Goodrich for my elder son. The myth was of particular interest to me because my mother was born in Czechoslovakia, and her mother, in Hungary. I had a great-great aunt named Berta. The moment I started reading, I was hooked.

The Berta myth was first written down by a Belgian minstrel, Adenes li Rois, Little Adam, King of Minstrels, in 1270. He was a true virtuoso at his art – his poem consists of 3,482 verses. I depended on Goodrich's rendition of the story, since his poem has never been translated. Adenes li Rois deals with events that transpired in eighth-century France – the marriage of Princess Berta of Hungary to Pepin the Short of

France. They eventually became the parents of Charlemagne.

The story concerns an evil servant, Margiste, who substitutes her own daughter, Aliste, for Berta in the bridal bed. The two girls greatly resemble each other, save for the size of their feet. Berta is known historically as Berta Broadfoot; perhaps she was clubfooted or had exceptionally large feet. Margiste orders Berta to be slain in the woods of Le Mans. Unbeknownst to Margiste, Berta escapes. The heart of a wild boar is brought back to Margiste as proof of Berta's death. The King lives with Aliste. She bears him two sons. For seven years, Pepin is unaware of the hoax. Here are the roots of two fairy tales, eleven hundred years before the Brothers Grimm: Cinderella (whose distinguishing characteristic is her tiny feet, as opposed to Berta's large ones) and Snow White (whose stepmother rivals Margiste in cunning and selfishness).

Indeed, the mother-daughter relationship is explored in depth throughout the myth. Berta, the true Queen, has a loving (good) mother in Queen Blancheflor of Hungary. Aliste, the servant girl who lives the part of Queen, has a ruthless, domineering mother. As I developed the story, I decided the two girls should share the same father, King Floire of Hungary. This would account for their physical resemblance and for Margiste's bitterness toward Berta. Margiste was supposedly Queen Blancheflor's most trusted servant.

Margiste is the ambitious mother who lives vicariously through her daughter, exploiting her for her own purposes. Yet there is a quality of the heroic about Margiste – she is absolute in her strivings. She never swerves, never relents, never regrets. And Aliste? She is shrewd, yet disconsolate at being forced to live a lie. She is alternately passive and aggressively demanding. At the core, there is only one thing she desires but never wins: the unconditional regard and affection of her mother. Thus we have two mothers, Queen Blancheflor and Margiste, and two daughters, the half-sisters Berta and Aliste.

Although it was the ramifications of these relationships that first intrigued me, I soon became curious to know what was 'true' in the historical sense. I found Pepin the Short readily enough in the history books. Imagine my excitement when I came to my first reference to Berta Broadfoot. I found no reference to either Margiste or Queen Blancheflor. One source said Berta didn't actually marry Pepin until Charlemagne was old enough to 'walk down the aisle'. Other sources remark that Charlemagne was unusually devoted to his mother.

Two books which were especially helpful in describing the food, clothing, customs and laws of the time were *France in the Middle Ages: Customs, Classes and Conditions* by Paul Lacroix (New York: Ungar Publishers, 1963) and *Daily Life in the World of Charlemagne* by Pierre Riché (Pennsylvania: University of Pennsylvania Press, 1978). These books stimulated the birth of additional characters who might breathe some life into the facts – the hermit, the soothsayer (a dream analyst of the time), and my favorite scoundrel, the pilgrim. The minor characters allowed me to range far afield, since I was finding these distant medieval times amazingly vital. I discovered that there were sewage systems in monasteries; thus Pepin could write his elder brother Carloman, who had retreated to the monastery at Monte Cassino, to 'bathe' frequently. Monks who were over-zealous in their attempts to purify themselves ceased bathing. It is an historical fact that Carloman entered this monastery under mysterious circumstances, ceding his portion of land to his younger brother, Pepin, enabling Pepin to extend his kingdom.

After I read of the complex and intricate medieval methods

of torture, I knew my fictional Executioner (Le Maistre des Haultes Oeuvres) would be a rather dull-witted bureaucrat who chafed under the lack of respect paid to him by other government dignitaries. Being an ambitious fellow, he would quite naturally desire to move to a land where he would be held in higher esteem (Bavaria).

It is difficult for us to imagine the great and immense woods that once covered the face of Europe. The perils of famine, pestilence, frequent warfare, and wild beasts, led some men to withdraw entirely from human society – to live as hermits. My version of the hermit is a man obsessed with the mathematically precise formulas of metaphysical distance which characterized the view of the universe at that time. He is the sexually repressed statistician who shuns human contact.

The status of women also interested me. Since the men were so frequently absent for extended periods, engaged in warfare or servitude to the nobility, women quite often managed their estates, down to the most minute detail.

Life was so tenuous, so chaotic, that a complex legal system developed, one that took a rather tolerant attitude toward alcohol. If one committed certain crimes while 'in one's cups', the penalties (usually monetary) were less severe than if one committed crimes in 'cold blood'. Thus, the mendacious pilgrim.

For a period of months, these minor characters sprang into existence. I never knew who would be born next. Some of my major characters were silent during this time. I had no idea where I was going, or how all these characters were going to fit into the whole. I had no sense of the whole. Certainly, the series was not written in sequence. I began to gain a clearer insight into Pepin. I imagined him a politician and military general of exceptional merit – a man of action rather than one of insight or introspection. He would be so absorbed in the ruling of his kingdom that he would only feel a slight disappointment in his relationship with his wife. A character who eluded me, Aliste, did not become fully developed until two years after I thought I had completed the series, perhaps indicating a reluctance to confront the 'bad' in me. I knew Berta, the Lady, but who was the Chambermaid? She had to both love and envy her half-sister, and to feel guilt at betraying her. It became clear to me that she was a pawn of her mother's ambitions, perhaps playing out Margiste's own wish to be the legitimate Queen.

The essential conflicts inherent in the story of Berta and Pepin are timeless. While customs and cultures may change, verities of character and motivation do not.

B.G.

Characters

PRINCESS BERTA OF HUNGARY (BERTA BROADFOOT), daughter of Queen Blancheflor and King Floire of Hungary. Marries King Pepin the Short of France, 741 A.D.

KING PEPIN THE SHORT OF FRANCE, son of Charles Martel. First King of the Franks to be annointed by the Pope (753 A.D.).

CARLOMAN, Pepin's older brother, a brave knight who entered a monastery under mysterious circumstances, renouncing his land and inheritance.

MARGISTE, trusted servant to Queen Blancheflor. Accompanies Berta to France in order to see her safely married, and to become her personal servant.

ALISTE, Margiste's daughter. Illegitimate daughter of King Floire of Hungary. Bears a great physical resemblance to Berta, save for the size of her feet.

HOLY HERMIT, lives in the forest of Le Mans.

PILGRIM

SOOTHSAYER

LE MAISTRE DES HAULTES OEUVRES, Executioner to King Pepin.

Table of Contents

Prologue: Margiste Reveals 17
Berta Remembers Childhood Games With Aliste 19
Queen Blancheflor Bids Berta Farewell 20
Berta Reflects On Her Wedding Day 22
Margiste Feigns A Great Concern 25
Aliste Considers Her Position 27
Letter From Pepin To His Elder Brother Carloman
At The Monastery Of Monte Cassino 29
Berta Survives Her Ordeal
And Finds Refuge In Illuminations 32
On Why The Holy Hermit Turned Beauty Away
When She Beat Upon His Door 34
King Pepin Addresses His Troops
Before Combat With The Lombards 35
The Pilgrim States His Case Before The Bishop 37
The Soothsayer Is Summoned To Interpret
Blancheflor's Dream 41
Aliste Agrees To Take Poison In Order
To Counterfeit An Illness 43
King Pepin Laments His Betrayal 45
Aliste Speaks With Double Tongue 49
Margiste Protests 51
Margiste's Desire 52
Le Maistre Des Haultes Oeuvres Reports To The King 53
Le Maistre Des Haultes Oeuvres Reports To Aliste 55
Aliste Bids Her Son Adieu 58
King Pepin Commences His Search For The True Queen 60
Pepin Sees Beauty And Advises Her Not To Be Alarmed 61
Queen Blancheflor Breaks The Seal
Of King Pepin's Missive 62
Berta Converses With God In Her Bath 63

Prologue: Margiste Reveals

But listen. It is an old tale.
A maiden is switched for a maiden
in the bridal bed. In the dark
who can tell? A man is a man
and humps for his own release.
The dark is dark. Does he look
at the feet? Only a mother knows
her child by the feet. Berta,
Debonaire, was quick to believe
that Pepin would come with a knife.
I disrobed Aliste in her stead.
And Berta, gagged by a rope, smothered
in cloth, was led to the lonely
dark forest of Mans. We thought all
was well. Aliste chirped like a bird,
levied taxes on pepper, cumin and wax.
We should have fled to Sicily.
Pepin twists my thumbs with screws.
I confess! I confess all! Even
the dagger, even the poison, no regrets!
A great fire is kindled with thorns.

Berta Remembers Childhood Games With Aliste

At the edge of the forest pretending
we were pigs snuffling for acorns
under the oak trees, under an oak

she wrestled me to the ground, pricked
my thumb with a thistle. We are
sisters, she whispered. Laughing

I called her my wild cornelian cherry.
She lifted my skirts and whispered,
Sister. Bloodroot. Little radish.

Queen Blancheflor Bids Berta Farewell

Daughter, be merry! What is this
talk of knives? As the apple
falls from the tree, so
must you take your leave from me.

At this moment, Pepin and France
await you, every street in Paris
festooned with banners.

Do not be hasty in copying
the dress of foreigners,
with bodices that open
at the hips, or hanging
sleeves. Be mindful
of the hem of your cloak.

Inform yourself on the number
of oxen, sheep, cows on your estate,
the fruits from your orchards.
Keep the medicinal herbs free
from troublesome weeds.

On your nuptial eve, bathe
in rose-water, sweeten
your breath with anise.
When Pepin comes in all firmness,
raise high your limbs to hasten
the journey of his seed.

May you be blessed with sons!
Spare them the vice of idleness.
Should you bear daughters, may
they nourish you as you
have nourished me, sweet
contignac of my heart.

Care for Margiste: she stands
in for me. Arrange
for her daughter Aliste
to be well-married in France.
Ransomed from slavery from
my own pocket, they will serve you
faithfully, I am certain.

Here is your bay palfrey.
Let all of France cry,
'Have we a springtime mistress!'

Berta Reflects On Her Wedding Day

i. The Hawks

The King is beside himself. From the Abbott
a wedding gift: six white hawks, miraculous!
He races to find a red cloth lure, stuffed
with chicken hearts. The birds, released,
attack the lure, hearts fall out, disappear.

The falconer covers the hawks with leather
hoods, fastens to claws golden rings inscribed
with these words: 'I belong to the King.'

I saw it once, a man accused of stealing
birds. Ravenous beaks allowed to feast
on human flesh, his bloodied chest. I hear
it still, piercing screams, as bells retreat
to open sky. Off to one side, the hawk-dealer
stood, yawning and satisfied.

ii. The Tapestry

The Abbott has not forgotten me: a sumptuous
tapestry of the Lady in the Garden. Her
handmaiden kneels at her feet in shimmering
emerald green, as Aliste kneels before me now,
painting my toenails and chattering.

I have ordered the tapestry hung from the East
window. Griffon and deer blaze up in silk,
perfect and diminutive. I could lie down

in that crimson field, bare my breast
to the crimson sky. And all around
the ripening smell of apples and muscadel.

iii. Reflections

I never cared for birds, neither *oiseaux*
de poing, nor *oiseaux de leure.* I prefer
the lyre, its measured notes, to songbirds.
Yet I adore my Pekinese, fidelity based
on love, not the scent of bloodied quail.
What nature of beast my new husband?

For sixteen years I have been your daughter.
Soon I shall be wife and queen. I am drawn
to the Lady, target for the enchanted arrow.
They say this arrow never misses its mark,
can reach game from extraordinary distances.
Birds of prey see a hare's whiskers from
extraordinary heights. Mother, how can I
explain? It's not that my heart didn't race
when Pepin took my hand, but rather
I feel an extraordinary distance
from the only self I have ever known.

Margiste Feigns A Great Concern

Madam! My child! I tremble
to tell you this: it is said
when Pepin comes this night
to do his Kingly duty, he
comes armed with a knife.

Lady, no use weeping. After
abbots and bishops bless
the bridal bed, I'll place
Aliste in your stead. If
one's to be murdered, let
it be she. You know what
your mother did for me.

Cursed be men, their lust
and their terrible greed.
Hand over your ruby cabochon
and the deception's complete.

Aliste Considers Her Position

Who was there to turn to when I found
his morning gift, a handsome brooch
encrusted with pearls, on my pillow?
Him? Not him, no morning gift, pink
and strutting, boasting of the seed
he felt spring from him with the force
of ten thousand steeds. When he forced
himself on me, pink, boastful, bent
to suckle like a piglet in his greed,
who was there? He threw his head back,
shouted, boasting of his seed, my morning
gift, and who was there to turn to? I set
my lips in imitation of a smile, spread
my limbs like any sow, but who was there?
Could I proclaim, pink and strutting, 'This.
This is who I am, your morning gift, servant
girl who cannot sign her name. And do you
love her still? Would you leave a gift,
a morning gift, a handsome brooch, on her
pillow?' Who was there, who, to turn to?

Not Mother, hopping about with glee, fingers
greasy from palace meat. She pokes my ribs
and cackles, 'We fooled him, eh? We two
make quite a team.' We two make quite a team
when, hankering for all I've lost, I think
of home and sister and the poor dumb sheep
I used to shear. Sister. Sister. Poor
dumb sheep I used to shear. Berta and I
once laughed ourselves asleep. I shuddered
when I saw her heart, darkly gleaming in

Mother's palm. She hopped about with glee
then tossed it down her throat. 'There,'
she said. 'That's done,' her fingers greasy
from the meat. And poked my ribs, while I,
dumb sheep, play the part of Queen. Berta
and I, we could have made a team. And laughed
ourselves asleep. I've thought of claiming
defect of consent, *diriment impediment,* but
Mother would be lost for good, poor sheep.
Since there is no one human I can turn to,
I turn with more than human need to the feel
of silk, darkly gleaming, next to my skin.

Letter From Pepin To His Elder Brother Carloman At The Monastery Of Monte Cassino

My beloved brother,
At last a moment between petitions
to take up pen and write to you,
who are dearest in my heart. I grieve
today because my horse, most faithful
companion in hunt and battle, has fallen,
not by sword or arrow, but from ignominious
disease. When I saw the blood flow from his lips,
I myself thrust in the sword, and tears flowed
from my eyes. He cannot be replaced, but
I have entrusted Gaudiocus with forty sous
to buy the palomino stallion I so admired
at Ardennes. I suppose in time I shall
be able to mount him with a flying leap,
in the meantime, I mourn. As I mourn
your absence. To think of you poring
over manuscripts when once you pierced
many a helmet, broke many a hauberk,
cut off many an enemy's head. How valiant
you were, second to none! I have never
understood your decision, to renounce
all that, as well as the sparrow hawks
and the falcons. Not to mention maidens
in their first bloom!

Berta is well, although, just like a woman,
she does nothing but speak of bolts of silk
from Pavia. A wife costs dearly, Carloman,
to keep them gentle. Last week nothing less
than an otter cloak could unpinch her lips,

loosen her thighs. And now she croons to me
morning and night about silk, silk.

My liver troubles me. I find a spoonful
of honey, vinegar, mustard and ten grains
of pepper soothing. A recent diversion
was a visit from the Ambassador of Baghdad.
A hunt with full clamor for aurochs. How
the Asiatics fear wild oxen! Heudris,
my younger son, stamped his feet until
I consented to let him watch from a hillock.
But Rainfrois, I fear, shall never be a hunter.
He clings to his mother well past the age
in such matters. She dotes on him, fosters
his unmanliness. Remember when I faced that
lion, disembowelled him in a twinkling with my sword?
How proud our mother was! Would that all my time
could be spent hunting and fighting, but alas,
there are always affairs of state and endless
details to attend to – appeasing the Pope,
our half-brother Grifo a constant thorn
in my side. He tries to incite the Saxons.
And can you imagine? A mere hogshead of oats
costs a whole denier.

Dear brother, do not become ascetic.
Consent to warm yourself and to bathe.
I imagine you with a parchment
under your arm, a cowl over your head.
Remember me in your prayers.

Berta Survives Her Ordeal
And Finds Refuge In Illuminations

After the ground shook with the thud
of hooves, and they left me trembling
in my white chemise, rain began to fall,
whipped by an icy wind. I stumbled through
the forest, tripping over slippery stones,
my arms scratched by low-hanging branches.
Lightning flashed, revealed an opening –
I darted down one path, then another,
but soon was lost in a maze of trees.
How dense those woods were, and how forsaken.
Owls hooted from treetops, wolves howled
in the distance. 'Saint Denis!' I cried out,
'I am lost! Saint Catherine! Save me!'
I sped wearily on, my dress torn and ragged,
until I found a hollow spot, laid my sorrows
at God's feet, and chilled and lost as I was,
I slept.

When I awoke, blue from cold, I prayed, 'Sir God,
show me where to go and henceforth I will be humble.
I will never tell who I am, not that I am the daughter
of Hungary, nor the wife of France. Grant that I
may keep my maidenhood. And may Margiste suffer
a horrible death!' God led me to a holy hermit
who showed me the path to Simon and Constance.

Sooner than I like to think, life became quite ordinary.
The ordinary crust of bread, the ordinary courtesies.
Those sturdy, upright people accepted me, a stranger
with no trace of past. They marveled at my modesty,

while inwardly I longed for throne and kingly caresses.
Daily I read in my psalter. How glorious the illuminations,
the Madonna's robe a brilliant blue from lapis-lazuli,
and carmine from the little ilex beetle.
From my Book of Hours, the haymakers in June
formed a backcloth to the gaudy lives of nobles
making love in May. Years passed. I began to sense
the power which comes from guarding a secret vow, long
past its earthly usefulness. By granting all to God,
I maintained sovereignty over my own will.

Praise God in all His generosity. The more
arduous the keeping of my vow, the more regal
and full of circumstance, my rule.

On Why The Holy Hermit Turned Beauty Away When She Beat Upon His Door

There came a time in my life when all
I craved was order: the exact dimensions
of the Earth's diameter, facts a stay
against famine and war. The moon
is 39 times smaller than our planet,
the sun 166 times larger. To be sure
it is difficult to speak of the stars,
so far away that if a stone were thrown
from one, it would take 100 years to land
near this hut (at the rate of 74¼ milles
per hour). If I were to walk at the rate
of 25 milles per day, it would take me
7,157½ years to reach the stars. Less
time is needed for a good soul after death
to arrive at Heaven – under half-an-hour
to be precise.

And this only speaks of distance.
What of the beaver who severs its testicles
in order to escape the hunter? So I
(a holy hermit) would triumph over temptation.
Consider the fate of the antelope – captured
when its needle-sharp horns become entangled
in a bush. 'Beauty,' I told her, 'I can let
no fiend in, neither in summer nor winter.'
She was the Devil come to tempt me, what else
was Beauty doing in these leafy woods? I passed
her a piece of bread through the wicket, told her
the path to the home of Simon the Sheriff. God
is my judge. I must beware the Infernal Hunter
who seeks to impale the souls of men.

King Pepin Addresses His Troops Before Combat With The Lombards

You have obeyed my command to fast and pray
for three days in barefoot procession. Warriors,
we are like the Old Testament Maccabees!
Soon we sing a holy canticle, the Kyrie
Eleison, then we plunge into combat!

Those who sold arms to merchants and used
the money for drink were condemned to water
for the campaign's duration. Prove stout
in battle, and a flagon of wine from the King's
cask! Those who pillaged before the enemy's
land was reached have been held accountable,
even for breaches committed by your horses.
Now let us move as one body in our massive charge!

We have in our possession the finest war machines:
rams, catapults, rolling towers. Batter the walls
on every side. Flood the province, ferret
out the living hiding in woods or concealed
in ditches. Imagine how unreservedly you may give
yourselves up to the joys of looting! We shall fly
the autumn vineyards like serried ranks of thrushes
pecking at grapes. We have fifteen carts, drawn
by four bulls each, to be filled with gold and silver.
There are swords here of Indian origin.
How our women will applaud us! But first, turn
the fields white with linen habits of the dead.

Soldiers, prepare yourselves! Feel the smooth
shaft of lance, your quivers full of arrows. Bless

your sword, call it by name, raise it as a cross
between your hands. Do not abandon your horse,
even for the life of your mother. His reins
must not be gripped by any wretch but you!

Fetch the military almoner! Bow before the bishop's
chant of three masses and three psalms: one for the King,
one for this Frankish army, and a third
for the present situation. To arms! To arms!
No greater hunt than the hunt of men!

The Pilgrim States His Case Before The Bishop

I am a pilgrim in search of wonders. I have seen fragments from the Holy Cross and tattered bits from the Holy Coat. I was at Mozac when the chapel was so crowded that women wailed as though in childbirth. I escaped with my life by walking on the worshippers' heads.

The best prostitutes are to be found near chapels. Last night a prostitute tricked me into going to her home with the oldest ploy in the world: she claimed to know me from childhood.

The life of a pilgrim is too great a hardship for a man with family. It is best to travel alone.

My beloved wife is barren. That is why I visit so many towns and worship the remains of the apostles.

Yes, I know the recipe for maleficciuum. Doesn't everyone? One mixes a potion from fern roots, willow leaves, rue, gillyflower seeds and saffron. But I have never administered such a potion to one with child.

I slept at the hostelry last night. It was crowded with pilgrims come to visit the boy's grave. Tomorrow is Good Friday, the anniversary of his miraculous death.

Last night I spent some time in the tavern. The wine here is unusually sour.

The laws in this town are just. There are allowances made if one commits certain crimes while in one's cups.

The sheriff Simon invited me to his home last night. During

the day I had helped him trap a poacher.

There are many lovely maidens in this town. Not just the three who reside with Simon and Constance.

Most of the women in this town are old, with flesh like pudding. I have a distaste for women who sprout hair from moles on their chins.

I have thought of becoming a monk. The rule of chastity would be easier for me to obey than the rule of silence.

Simon's adopted daughter Berta was rude to me when I complimented her on her embroidery. Aiglente and Ysobel were happy to launder my shirt. No, I never pulled off her headdress.

Life in some towns is so tedious. Great crowds will gather just to see a dog run frantically with a pan tied to its tail.

I have been to the Island Taprobane, the true terrestial Paradise. Each year it has two winters and two summers.

You are fortunate to have such reliquaries in this town. They ensure revenue for the populace, and many pilgrims who will dazzle you with tales from afar while you sit in the safety of your chair.

How does a town begin? Four crosses are placed at the cardinal points. Trace out the limits, build church, town hall, market place, squares, streets. Then give it a name: Neuville, Villeneuve, Neufchateau, Villefranche.

I did not lift the maiden's skirt. I did not lift it to the calf. I did not lift it to the knee. I did not force her to remove her garments. I am more tempted by sweetcakes than by women.

I was with a prostitute last night, as I told you.

I was at the tavern last night, as I told you.

I merely had dinner with Simon and Constance last night, as I told you.

It is true I travel widely, but I have a wife and six children in the town of Villefranche.

I most reluctantly agree to pay a fine of forty sous. Perhaps I did touch her headdress, but only as a gesture of friendship. I most emphatically did not touch her elsewhere.

I plan to depart immediately. Please accept my donation of forty sous for the care of the reliquary. A cup of water would be most appreciated. I am not used to the wine in this town.

The Soothsayer Is Summoned
To Interpret Blancheflor's Dream

i. The Dream

In this dream the dreamer knows
she is dreaming. Holds a wide-
toothed comb in her hand. Soft
thump at door. Enter a bear.
She pulls comb through dark fur.
Strong odor of musk, honey,
cloves. Dreamer sings lulla,
lullaby, go to sleep my plump
sweet. Bear sucks on paw.
Paw becomes raking claw.
Tears cheek, rips right arm,
begins to gnaw at dreamer's
rib-cage. Scatters bones on floor.
Dreamer finds mirror. Torso
a carcass. Right arm dangles
from its socket. Face half-
gone. Bear sees bear. Mirror
mirror. Bear bear. Thump thump.

ii. The Interpretation

I bind phylacteries with ribbons
to my arms, with cords to my legs.
Combine letters of dreamer's name.
I climb to the rooftop, pay heed
to the direction of smoke. Examine
the excrement of a cat. Study
the sky. Make note that moon
in fourth quarter. Omen of death.
Comet appears in sign of Scorpio.
Open book at random. Scrutinize
all data. Interpretation: extreme
danger to dreamer's daughter. Long
voyage required. Dreamer pulls hair
in lamentation. There is no pleasure
to such work.

Aliste Agrees To Take Poison
In Order To Counterfeit An Illness

Mother, pull your cushion closer,
I am afraid because of my feet.
Let us load the mules and flee.
I am weary of pretense, and Italian
winters are mild.

This being Queen, Mother, was never
for me. I could have married a rich
man, with jewels enough for three.
There is a hunger in you that I
could never satisfy.

I used to think it was Berta
you really loved. Why so
surprised? When you fussed
over her toilette, whatever
crumb she placed inside her mouth?

Now I see nobility quickens
your breath, brings a flush
to your cheeks. Perhaps you
desire yet another King, hard
as a hammer, to leap in your bed!

Forgive me, Mother, for I am faint
with fear. Bells ring at Montmartre,
herald the arrival of Queen Blancheflor.
No force on earth will keep her
from storming the royal bedchamber.

There. I have eaten your poisoned
pear. Do you still accuse me
of lacking nerve? We are bound
together by more than love. Pray
this illness will not prove fatal.

Hold me, Mother. The bells ring.
Doom's icy fingers circle my throat.
I am afraid because of my feet.
Have you laced the pear with poison?
There is still time to load the mules.

King Pepin Laments His Betrayal

My dearest brother.
Oh rage, oh calumny, oh most
unspeakable horror! The Queen
is not the Queen, my wife is not
my wife, but a clever cut-purse
who performed her art with skill
and dexterity. Fooled by a woman,
robbed by a woman, attacked
by a woman, defiled by a woman!
My head reels when I contemplate
my grievous wrong. I am a cuckoo,
far removed from its usual source
of merriment.

I wanted to stone the woman I thought
my wife, but was advised to spare
the mother of my children (though
sight of their rosy cheeks appalls
me!). She groveled at my feet, a common
mongrel, pleading, 'Remember our nights
together in bed!' Carloman, so many
feverish nights I plowed with fury
into that most devious furrow!
A taste of bile rushes to my lips.

I have cast her off. At dawn
she departs for the convent at Montmartre.
Wagons groan under the weight of silk
and precious gems I lavished on her,
gold and silver she gained through illegal
taxation. All will be distributed to the poor,

small recompense for the years my people
were deprived of a true Queen. My soul
is sorely troubled. And am I not a man?
I remember our nights together in bed.

Tonight I shall ignore the penitentials
and dedicate myself to Bacchus, easing
my throat with the best Moselle.
Remember after battling the Avars,
how we devoted ourselves to a drinking
bout, both too proud to call a halt
until the floor became a bed for us?
Eia! What good my military victories
if my own hearth be in chaos? Carloman,
you alone are faithful to me. Where
are the loaded dice we used to sport
with? Are you truly content with relics
and holy water? I need your presence
to keep my nails from tearing my face!

Aliste Speaks With Double Tongue

I couldn't stand
I couldn't sit
I paced, a wild thing
until he stormed
in my bedchamber,
struck me down. How
could I after all
our nights together in bed
grabbing me, scratching my face
my breasts, his tears staining
his cheeks. 'Lost!' he cried
and I did fear for him
ardent in rage, rising,
I think he must
love that girl
departing now on horseback

this fact: they were torturing her
I could hear her shrieks
she couldn't save me now
but who was there, who
to save me, strike me down.
How could I, over and over
save her? I was her prisoner
caught in deceit. I couldn't
protect her, she couldn't protect
me, unbearably alone. I clung to,
clinging to the bedpost. Mother! I cried
for Mother. The flames
the smell of scorched flesh
never never cease to
blame her, her ambition
now reduced to ash.

Margiste Protests

If I were a man they would sing
of my daring, call me Margiste the Bold.
No lioness did more for her cub. Gladly
I'd give my scarlet hose for a song
of my daughter, Aliste of the Narrow Feet.
Instead they sing of Bert aus Grans Pies,
Bertha Broadfoot, Berta the Debonaire.
Why should *she* have been Queen of France,
were both girls not blonde, not fair?
Both dimpled, both winsome, both mantled
with golden hair? Both sired by Hungarian
King Floire? (His wife, Blancheflor, so noble,
so pure, she always gave to a fault to the poor.)
Berta was Highborn, Aliste a mere serving girl.
Yet for eight years she played Queen to Pepin
the Short. He was well-satisfied.
My cousin Tibert (incompetent dolt)
swore that Berta was slain. I piss
on Berta! I piss on her big feet! Fooled
by a pig's heart! Burned for bearing a girl
with narrow feet! I don't care a mint leaf
what Pepin calls me now ('old hag, the Antichrist').
He once covered my daughter from evening till dawn.
Let them kindle for me a great fire with thorns!

Margiste's Desire

Even now the flames are hot. Even now
the flames are white. I pray my death
is swift. I did it all for Aliste.
To be burned for bearing a girl
with narrow feet! Sing of me,
sing the song of Margiste!

Le Maistre Des Haultes Oeuvres Reports To The King

As the King's Sworn Tormentor, I am bound
to inform you of events that transpired
to the old woman you placed in my charge.
As you instructed, the following preparatory
tortures were administered: the usual twisting
of thumbs with screws, during which hot eggs
were placed under the armpits. According
to your fancy, goats were led in to avidly
lick her feet, which had been doused in salt
water. This proved a most effective agony.
Confession was immediately forthcoming.

You decreed her crime a capital offense:
execution by fire. The stake was erected
in the designated spot, the northern section
of the marketplace. The pile was carefully
prepared, as per the most efficient design:
layers of straw and wood were alternated
to the victim's height. Pains were taken
to leave a free space round the stake
and a passage that led to it. The victim's
body hair was shaved. She was stripped
of her clothing and dressed in a shirt
smeared with sulphur. She walked through
the narrow opening to the pile's center.
Ropes and chains tightly bound her
to the stake. Faggots and straw
were thrown into empty spaces until
she was entirely covered. The fire
was lit from all sides at once. Her body
was slowly devoured by flames.

When it was possible, I approached the center
of the burning pile, scooped a few ashes
in a shovel, sprinkled them into the air.
I am your most trusted servant, am always
at your disposal.

Le Maistre Des Haultes Oeuvres Reports To Aliste

Lady, I accept with thanks your gift
of one hundred gold sous. It is not
that I am without means: *havage*
from every load of grain, taxes
on sales of herring and watercress,
the fine of five sous levied on stray
pigs which is my due. There are rents
from shops and stalls surrounding
the pillory. Still, here an odium
is attached to my craft. Not so
in other lands. Here, I am forced
to wear a yellow coat. The Chancellor
threw my letters of appointment
under the table, a token of contempt.
Such is the source of my discontent.
Consider the services I provide:
execution by fire, sword, mechanical
force; administration of quartering,
the wheel, the fork, the gibbet,
drawing, spiking, cutting of ears,
dismembering, flogging, the pillory.
And my other services to the community:
one can buy fat from me of culprits
who have been hung, the medicinal value
of which is well-known. My expertise
in the setting of limbs. Enough.
I shall use your gift to apply
for a position in Bavaria, where
I will be treated with respect.

Now to assure you that your gift enabled
death to be swift and painless. I placed
a large and pointed bar amongst the faggots,
opposite the stake, breast high. This bar
impaled the unfortunate woman, delivering
a mortal blow, directly after the fire was lit.
Praise God I could spare her suffering.

Aliste Bids Her Son Adieu

One two three dandle
Rainfrois on my knee,
Four five six there
are some things Queens
can't fix:

Inside the *scrinia*
underneath the *peplum*,
fetch the eagle in filigree
and granulated gold. This
is the *fibula* I stole as a
sapling, I stole it from
Berta, from under her nose.
She cried, inconsolable,
until I took pity and
gave her a bite of my
aubergine fritter. She
kissed me with plum lips,
she loved me so. I dashed
to Margiste, my mother, you
grand-mère, whose shiny black
eyes glittered like olives.
She cuffed me at once, frowned
and inquired why I hadn't the
wits to have stolen the pair.
Sprawled in the mud like a
newborn calf in a fresh caul

of blood, dazed and alarmed,
I felt so alone. Choufleur,
the masquerade is done.

Six five four I am
heartsick to the core.
Three two one now
our sorrow is begun.

---

scrinia – hope chest
peplum – cloak, material
fibula – brooch used at shoulders
to fasten the robe

King Pepin Commences His Search For The True Queen

Carloman.
Quite right you are to remind me
that I am, indeed, the King.
All of France falls with me
if I yield to my deplorable shame.
I have given the order to search
each hectare of Le Mans. Eight
long years since Berta was abandoned
in that immense domain. I pray God
spared her the fangs of ravenous wolves.

I join this sacred hunt, but dressed
as knight. This day I do not feel kingly
enough to proclaim it to the woods.
If God sees fit to reunite us, I will not
be contained, will rapturously cover
her body with kisses! I say this to you,
my brother, not the monk you have become:
I am famished for my lost bride!

Pepin Sees Beauty And Advises Her Not To Be Alarmed

Feeling melancholic and out of sorts,
I left the hunting party, let my horse
lead me where he willed. We came upon
a chapel hidden in the woods, and there
was Beauty emerging. 'Beauty,' I said,
'don't be alarmed. I am knight and vassal
of the King to whom the whole of France
belongs. In truth, I've lost my way,
which pains me not a little. Could you
redirect me?' Blonde curls peeked
beneath her hood. Sky-blue eyes, crimson
cheeks, and suddenly, I was beside myself,
dismounted in a flash, pressed her to me
before she could even gasp. 'Love me,'
I breathed into her ear. 'Make love
to me. Any precious gem is yours.'
She struggled like a trepanned hare.
'Land then, I will settle a rich estate
upon you, honor you afterwards, only
answer my desire!' but still she kept
me from her. I pushed back her hood,
cupped the small mound of her breast.

Beauty replied with great distinctness:
'Sir Knight, I forbid you to touch me!
You have offended me greatly.' Tears
rolled down her cheeks. 'I am no ordinary
damsel, but wife of Pepin, King
of France, and daughter of the Hungarian
throne. Know I am the Queen of France!'

Queen Blancheflor Breaks The Seal Of King Pepin's Missive

Dearest Mother, Queen Blancheflor.
I hesitate yet race to write you!
I cannot bear to see you once more
disappointed, but while searching
through that forest cloak, Le Mans,
I came upon a maiden claiming
to be your daughter, my wife. I bid
you come most speedily to verify
her statement. In that regard, I send
three hundred stalwart knights
to vouchsafe your arrival.

I warn you, the maiden now is steadfast
in her denial that she is my lost bride.
She says she only claimed it to protect
herself from my advances (intended
with only the highest degree of friendship,
I assure you). Would she not be delirious
to hide her rank from me? Her guardian
suggests that perhaps she made some vow
while chilled and famished in the woods,
which now she fears to break, endangering
her salvation. If true, a most virtuous,
Highborn lady she is, not tempted by gold
nor the Kingdom of France. Come quick!
My heart leaps in my chest!

Berta Converses With God In Her Bath

Sir God, I was not prepared
for this, intemperate love
annihilating all restraint.
Here I lie in rose-water,
chewing seeds of anise!

After years of baking barley
bread, gathering twigs for
firewood, an everpresent
line of dirt was etched
beneath my fingernails.

No pallet on the beaten
floor, but massive bed
with silken sheets, far
from pleasures that I found
in sacred vows, embroidery.

I am greedy for the black figs
which are his eyes, the flowering
almond smoothness of his skin,
that pale pink mushroom, his
manhood in a state of rest.

When our energies are spent,
no strength to even lift
a wrist, I turn to lick
the salt-sweat from the
hollow of his neck.

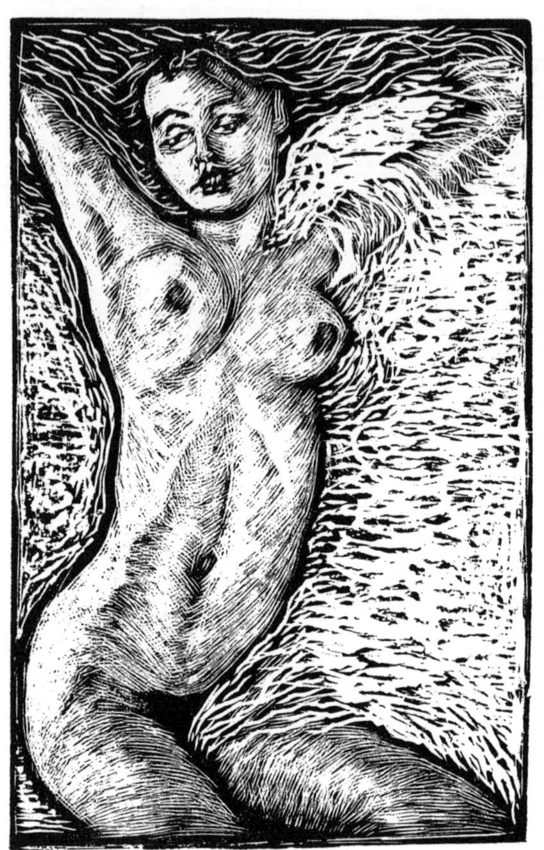

I know not if it be night or
day, or if the moon be full
or new, but only that I am
most blessed when he drinks
the warm wine of my womanhood.

King Pepin the Short of France
and Princess Berta of Hungary
became the parents of Charlemagne.

Bibliography

Castries, Duc de. *The Lives of the Kings and Queens of France.* Trans. Anne Dobell. New York: Knopf, 1979.

Chamberlin, E. R. *Life In Medieval France.* London: B.T. Batsford Ltd., 1967.

Evans, Joan. *Life In Medieval France.* London: Phaedon Press, 1957.

Goodrich, Norma Lorre. *Medieval Myths.* New York: New American Library, 1977.

Harthan, John. *The Book of Hours.* New York: Park Lane, 1977.

Huyghe, René. *Larousse Encyclopedia of Byzantine and Medieval Art.* General Editor. New York: Excalibur Books, 1981.

Lacroix, Paul. *France in the Middle Ages: Customs, Classes and Conditions.* New York: Ungar Publishers, 1963.

Lamb, Harold. *Charlemagne: The Legend and the Man.* New York: Doubleday and Co., 1954.

Riché, Pierre. *Daily Life in the World of Charlemagne.* Trans. Jo Ann McNamara. Pennsylvania: University of Pennsylvania Press, 1978.

PATRICIA BARROW

BARBARA GOLDBERG, raised in Forest Hills, New York, has degrees from Mount Holyoke College, Columbia University and The American University, Washington, D.C. where she received her M.F.A. and currently teaches Creative Writing. She has received a Fellowship from the National Endowment for the Arts and a grant from the Maryland State Arts Council. She won the first Word Works Washington Prize, has twice won the PEN Syndicated Fiction Project Competition and was the finalist in the Pablo Neruda Poetry Contest. Her full length poetry manuscript, *Cautionary Tales,* has been a finalist in the 1985 and 1986 National Poetry Series, The Walt Whitman Award, and others. Her work has appeared in *Poetry, The American Scholar, New England Review / Breadloaf Quarterly, Washington Review,* and others. The composer Judith Shatin Allen is presently working on a vocal quartet based on *Berta Broadfoot and Pepin the Short.* Goldberg lives in Bethesda, Maryland with her husband and two sons.

ROSS STANSFIELD

ROSEMARY FEIT COVEY had her first show at the age of twenty-four in New York City at Martin Sumers Graphics. Since then, she has had one-woman shows at the Folger Shakespeare Library, galleries in Washington, D.C., Geneva, Zurich and Buenos Aires. *American Artist* published a feature story, 'Rosemary Covey's Graphic Response to Emotions' in its July, 1986 issue. Her work has appeared in *Poetry, Gargoyle,* Piedmont Airlines inflight magazine, and others. Her prints have been selected for national juried shows, including a purchase award in the Manhattan National Print Show and the 'Man and Beast' exhibit at the Museum of American Art in Washington, D.C. Her work as an illustrator includes commissions from *The New York Times, The Washington Post,* The Washington Times Corp., the Xerox Corporation, the Republican Senatorial Committee, the International Federation of Metal Workers, and others. In 1980 she completed an edition of the Belle of Amherst for Julie Harris in her role as Emily Dickinson. Born in South Africa, Covey was educated at Cornell University and the Maryland Institute of Art. She currently lives in Alexandria, Virginia and has her studio at the Torpedo Factory Art Center.